In loving memory of Josette.

—M.G.

I'd like to thank my daughter Amelia, whose love and compassion
for dogs (and all creatures great and small) were a real inspiration
during the making of this book. Thanks to Sarah Hokanson of Random
House for the book's beautiful layout and look. And lastly, thanks to
Jane Lahr for her enthusiasm and perseverance in getting it all done.

—R.Z.

Robert Rahway Zakanitch

is a fine artist who lives and works in New York City.
He was awarded a Guggenheim Foundation Grant,
and his work is represented in many public
collections, including the Philadelphia Museum
of Art, the Denver Art Museum, and the Whitney
Museum of American Art in New York.

Zakanitch created the paintings for this book as
an extension of his "Aggressive Goodness Series" of
large-scale dog portraits, whose unabashed purpose
was to evoke the notion of goodness and to remind
people of their aptitude for compassion.

Maya Gottfried spent many happy

hours with the portraits in this collection, absorbing
what Mr. Zakanitch—and each dog!—had to say, and
creating poems to express those sentiments. Her
first book for children was *Last Night I Dreamed
a Circus,* also illustrated by Mr. Zakanitch. She
lives in Brooklyn, where she is surrounded by
many inspiring good dogs.

GOOD DOG

y Maya Gottfried

ert Rahway Zakanitch

ED A. KNOPF   NEW YORK

Sit

Stay

Fetch

Heel

Lie down

Roll over

Shake hands

Speak

Jump

Run

Beg

Right away,

no problem,

whatever you say.

A dog's work is never done.

westie

Listen up! It's time to go.

Get the leash. Let's hit the road.

I've got a bone to pick with a Chihuahua,

And there's a coupla dachshunds that need a barking-to.

Put down your paper already,

let's get this show on the road.

Throw me my stick,

I'm ready to go.

MEMO
To: My Person
From: Your Little Friend
Re: My Apologies

I'm sorry about the stain on the piano bench. Accident,
won't happen again.
And my most sincere regrets about the hair on that nice wool suit.
I feel terrible about chewing on your custom-made leather shoes. Though,
they were on the floor.

PS: Have you seen my chew bone? I was sure that I'd left it on your pillow.

pekingese

I chased
that big dog,
over there,
I did.

Wait until
my owner's here.
He'll tell you like
it really is.

I chased that hound,
and then
he hid.

I may be small,
but I am swift.

Don't you mess with me.

CHIHUAHUA

Mmm, mmm, mmm, scratching behind my ear.

Chasing that duck across the grass.

Swooshing and splashing in the pond.

In the sun.

Running and running and running.

Digging in the warm, dry dirt.

Tired, resting on the big blanket.

Beside you.

Springer Spaniel

You did it again!

And you promised.

You promised!

A dog must GRRR! And ARF! And WOOF!

And chase and jump and frolic.

Look at me!

Hair! Hair! Hair! I can barely see!

Now I'm as round as a powder puff.

This is just embarrassing.

Pomeranian

Oh, throw me my plush tomato!

Then I will gladly lie down by your feet.

I've been here by the door since the sun disappeared,

awaiting the sound of your key.

Corgi

Do you take this dog to be your friend?

Will you see her through tangles and mats?

Through dog days and kennel stays?

Do you promise to put down your book

when she sits upon your lap?

And be faithful to her, and her alone?

As long as you both shall live?

I do.

maltese

All I really want is a hug and a bone.

Is that too much to ask?

Maybe it's the snout . . . or the snoring.

And the drool—well, it dries.

But you know, don't you? That

beneath this tough exterior there thumps a gentle heart.

BULLDOG

You aren't forgetting about dinner,
are you?

I know you were walking toward the door,
but you wouldn't leave without feeding me, would you?

There's a bag of food on the kitchen counter.
I could feed myself, you know, if you kept it on the floor.

For you, my dear, I will always be there.

I'll be in your dreams.

Curled up on your chair.

Through the dark night,

you need not be scared.

For you, only you,

I will always be there.

Oh yes, oh yes!
Well, first I went,
I went to the vet.
And yes, I was,
I was good.

And then, and then
we went to the park.
And yes, I ran.
I ran and ran!

And next, then next
I saw a cat!
And yes, I chased
and growled and barked.
I showed that cat!

So now! What now?
Oh yes, a kiss!
And still a scratch,
and then,
just then,
I'll lay
and
rest.

BOSTON TERRIER

Many times I've paced this hall,
searching for my missing ball.
Many times you heard me sigh
and told me, "It will be all right."
Three full times I circled round
before I finally settled down.

Borzoi

WHAT ARE YOU DOING IN MY CHAIR!?

There, now that I've resumed my throne,

perhaps you could fetch my royal rubber squeaky burger.

I'll forgive you this once,

but next time it's the doghouse for you.

King Charles Spaniel

Look at the field.

It's covered in snow.

See all my tracks!

The flakes on my nose.

Icy cold.

I don't care.

Let me dig

one more hole.

Then I promise I'll go back home.

scottie

Patches
Fido
Pooch
Petunia
Buddy
Queenie
Lucky
Rex

Rover
Spot
Champ
Thor
Luna

Who's a good dog?
Me.

THIS IS A BORZOI BOOK PUBLISHED BY ALFRED A. KNOPF

Text copyright © 2005 by Maya Gottfried
Illustrations copyright © 2005 by Robert Rahway Zakanitch
All rights reserved under International and Pan-American Copyright Conventions.
Published in the United States by Alfred A. Knopf, an imprint of Random House Children's
Books, a division of Random House, Inc., New York, and simultaneously in Canada by
Random House of Canada Limited, Toronto. Distributed by Random House, Inc., New York.
KNOPF, BORZOI BOOKS, and the colophon are registered trademarks of Random House, Inc.

www.randomhouse.com/kids

Library of Congress Cataloging-in-Publication Data
Gottfried, Maya.
Good dog / by Maya Gottfried ; paintings by Robert Rahway Zakanitch. — 1st ed.
p.   cm.
ISBN 0-375-83049-9 (trade) — ISBN 0-375-93049-3 (lib. bdg.)
1. Dogs—Juvenile poetry. 2. Dogs in art—Juvenile literature. 3. Children's poetry, American.
I. Zakanitch, Robert, 1935–, ill. II. Title.
PS3607.O87G66 2005
811'.6—dc22   2004015098

MANUFACTURED IN CHINA
10 9 8 7 6 5 4 3 2   January 2005   First Edition